How to Pray Salah

A Step-By-Step Guide to Connecting With Your Creator Through Islamic Prayer

Table of Contents

Introduction

In the Name of Allah, the Most Gracious, the Most Merciful, and by His blessing, we begin our book on Salah. May Allah (SWT) guide us and you to do good and honest deeds and to Jannah in the Hereafter.

Salah is the center of Islam. It is the second pillar of the Islamic faith, following the two Shahadahs (professions that There is no God but Allah and that Muhammad, May Peace Be Upon Him, is the messenger and servant of Allah). It is also the first thing a Muslim is asked about on the Day of Judgement. Prophet Muhammad (PBUH) is reported to say: *"The first of man's deeds for which he will be called to account on the Day of Resurrection will be Salah. If it is found to be perfect, he will be safe and successful; but if it is incomplete, he will be unfortunate and a loser."* Prophet Muhammad (PBUH) is also reported to say: *"Verily, between a man and unbelief, is abandoning the Salah."* Salah is when a Muslim goes out of their way five times a day, every day, to connect with their Creator, Allah (SWT).

Salah symbolizes the complete submission of a Muslim's will to Allah (SWT), especially in Sujud (prostration in English). Salah is mentioned in the Qur'an many times;

however, it was taught by the Prophet Muhammad (PBUH). Let's also remember that Salah is not a chore but a connection with Allah (SWT) and a shield from hellfire. So, let's learn about how to prepare for Salah.

Chapter 1: How to Prepare for Salah

First and foremost is intention; intention to perform Salah for Allah (SWT). We must all remember that Salah is not just a charade or series of movements performed a certain number of times. It is a period when you are standing in front of Allah (SWT), our one and only Creator. This calls for honesty in intention and truth in action. You don't pray Salah just because it is a mandatory prayer, but in seeking Allah's (SWT) satisfaction of Allah (SWT) and because it provides an escape from the hassle of daily life. It was narrated that Abu Ayyub said: "A man came to the Prophet (PBUH) and said: 'O Messenger of Allah, teach me and make it concise.' Muhammad (PBUH) responded: 'When you stand to pray, pray like a man bidding farewell. Do not say anything for which you will have to apologize. And give up hope for what other people have.' During Salah, you must concentrate on what truly matters; you must pray Salah with Khushu' (Reverence in English), for you are standing before Allah Almighty (SWT). Let's start with the first step, Wudu'.

Wudu'

Wudu' is the purification or ablution required by all Muslims before performing all Salawat (plural of Salah). Performing Wudu' is very simple.

1. *There is a certain process to ablution that is required before every prayer. Source: https://commons.wikimedia.org/wiki/File:Ablution_tap_in_Al-Ittihad_Mosque.JPG*

2. Intention

The first step is intention (niyyah in Arabic). We've also mentioned intention before, but why is it so important? Umar ibn al-Khattab reported that Prophet Muhammad (PBUH) said: "Deeds are but with intentions, and for the man is only what he intended. So, one whose emigration was to Allah and His Messenger (PBUH), then his emigration was to Allah and His Messenger (PBUH), and whoever emigrated to worldly benefits or to a woman to marry, his emigration would be to what he emigrated for." Good deeds aren't really good if they're not meant well, are they? For example, two people could spend their money feeding the poor. One intends his actions to please and satisfy Allah (SWT), and the other intends to show how good of a person they are. Whom do you think Allah (SWT) considers better? Therefore, it is important to be mindful during Wudu' and intend to do it for the sake of Allah (SWT).

3. In the Name of Allah the Most Gracious, the Most Merciful

After that, you should say, *"Bismillah Ar-Rahman Ar-Raheem,"* which means, "In the Name of Allah the Most Gracious the Most Merciful." Ideally, we should be saying this before all of our actions, for this is a very commendable act, as Prophet Muhammad (PBUH) is reported to say to Umar ibn Abi Salamah: "Mention Allah's Name (i.e., say Bismillah)." Saying *"Bismillah Ar-Rahman Ar-Raheem"* is fine out loud or silently in your heart. It also serves as an initiation for the purification of Wudu'.

4. Wash Your hands

It is a Sunnah (practice) of the Prophet Muhammad (PBUH) to wash his hands before Wudu'. It is optional to wash them once, twice, or thrice, although it is preferable to wash them three times. Start by washing your right hand thoroughly three times. Make sure the water reaches every part of your hand, leaving no dry spots. This includes removing anything on the skin like mud, nail polish, or anything similar that blocks the water from your skin or fingernails. After thoroughly washing your right hand, wash your left hand, preferably thrice as well, in the same manner, covering the spaces between your fingers and the nails.

5. Rinse Your Mouth Thrice

Now, for the first 'official' step of Wudu.' Cup your right hand and put some water in it. Then, rinse your mouth with this water. Move the water well around your mouth to cleanse it properly, and then spit it out. Do this three times.

6. Blow Your Nose Thrice

After that, take some water into your right hand and sniff it into your nostrils. Then, blow the water out. Do this three times, as well. The word 'sniff' is the closest translation of the word Istinshaq in Arabic. You could think of it as blowing your nose with a handful of water.

7. Wash Your Face Thrice

In this step, similar to washing your hands, nothing must cover your face. You must wash your entire face. From the top of your forehead to the bottom of your chin and from one ear to another. Not the ears themselves, though; these are in a later step. For men with a beard, run your fingers through your beard to wash it as you wash your face. Do this three times.

8. Wash Your Arms Thrice

Starting at your fingertips, wash your arms all the way to your elbows. Start with your right and then your left. Do this three times. Make sure your whole forearm and hand are all washed carefully, leaving no dry spots.

9. Wipe Your Head Once

Notice here that this step doesn't require full washing. You only need to wipe your head with your wet hands from the crown of your head – the highest point of the forehead – to the back of your head – right at the beginning of the back of your neck - and then return your hands from the back of your head to the crown again; one wipe back, and one wipe forward. Do this once. For people with long hair, as implied in the beginning, it is not necessary to ruffle the hair or wash it entirely. You only need to wipe your head from the crown to the bottom. It is narrated that Prophet Muhammad (PBUH) when doing Wudu', wiped his entire head from the crown to the back of the head without disturbing the hair. So, if your hair is long and you wish not to ruffle it, you may wipe from the crown of your head to the back without bringing your hands back.

10.   Wash Your Ears Once

Use your thumbs and index fingers to clean the outside and the inside of your ears with the same water you wiped your head with in the last step. You only need to do this once.

11. Wash Your Feet Thrice

For the final step, start at your toes and wash your feet from there to your ankle bones. Wash between the toes, the back of the ankle, and the heels; carefully wash your entire foot. Do this three times with your right foot and then three times with your left, making sure you leave no dry spots like before.

12. I Bear Witness

Now, you have completed your Wudu'. Following the Sunnah of the Prophet Muhammad (PBUH), you should say, *"Ash-hadu allaa ilaha illallah wa ash-hadu anna Muhammadan 'abduhu wa Rasuluh,"* this means "I Bear Witness that there is no God but Allah, and I bear witness that Muhammad is His servant and messenger."

After that, the Prophet (PBUH) would say the following Dua' (prayer i.e., asking Allah (SWT) for something): *"Allahuma j'alnee minat-tawwabeen waj'alnee minal mutatahireen,"* which means "O Allah, make me among those who seek repentance and make me among those who purify themselves." Now, you are ready to pray.

What Nullifies Wudu'

Now you might ask: "Should I do this before every Salah? How long does my Wudu' last?" The answer to this is simple. Wudu' is only nullified – i.e., you have to renew your Wudu' to pray – by the following things:

- Any natural discharge of the body: urine, stool, or passing gas.

- Falling asleep.

- Losing consciousness.

- Ejaculation; for both men and women.

A minor note: let's say you do wudu' before one prayer, and you pray the said prayer. Then, you stay until the time of the following prayer without meeting any of the nullifiers of Wudu'. You may go to pray directly. In other words, you don't have to do Wudu' before every Salah. One wudu' could last with you to two prayers, or three, or maybe all five of the day if you don't meet any of the above-mentioned nullifiers.

Wudu' with Socks or Shoes on

Let's say you did Wudu' once, and then you had to redo your Wudu', but this time you have socks on. You don't have to take them off. The sole difference is in step #10 (washing your feet). When you have your socks on during Wudu', instead of washing your feet three times, you gently wipe the top of your right foot with your right hand and then the same for your left foot, both with your right hand and over the sock. This applies to shoes or sandals as well, as long as they cover up to the ankles.

Note on Dressing

Salah is when a Muslim goes to stand before Allah (SWT), so it is preferable and commendable to wear the best clothes one has. Allah (SWT) says in Surah Al-A'raf chapter 7, verse 31 of the Holy Qur'an: "O Sons of Adam! Take your adornment at every mosque." Allah (SWT) urges his devoted worshippers to dress well when going to pray in mosques. However, you do not have to be formally dressed in a suit and tie or such. As for coverage, the Prophet Muhammad (PBUH) has instructed that men should be covered from the naval to the knee and preferably wear something that covers their shoulders. So, although not forbidden, tank tops are not preferable during Salah. Women, on the other hand, must cover all their bodies except the hands and the face.

Where to Pray

The place of prayer must be clean. You can pray on grass, sand, concrete, etc. If the place isn't clean, you can use a carpet or a prayer rug to cover the area where you will be praying. Mind that the place should not be too noisy or have too many people around. Try choosing a quiet and peaceful place. For example, if the time of prayer comes and you are sitting with your whole family in the living room with the TV on, you should go into a quieter room and get ready for your Salah. This allows for better Khushu', as distractions around you always take away your focus.

After finding a quiet place, face the Qiblah. From your location, the Qiblah of Islam is the direction of Kaa'bah in Makkah. Allah (SWT) commanded this directly in the Qur'an in Surah al-Baqarah chapter 2 verse, and He says: "We have already seen the turning about of your face to the heaven; so, We will indeed definitely turn you towards a Qiblah that shall satisfy you. So, turn your face towards the Sacred Mosque (the Mosque the Kaa'bah sits at the center of in Makkah), and (O Muslims), wherever you are, turn your faces in its direction."

When to Pray

In Islam, there are five daily mandatory prayers (Al-Salawat Al-Fara'id in Arabic). First is Fajr, prayed before dawn. Second is Dhuhr, prayed at noon. After that is Asr, prayed in the afternoon when an object's shadow is exactly as long as the object is. Maghrib comes next, prayed at sunset. Finally, Isha' is prayed at nightfall. Nowadays, calendars have precise timings on them, so you don't have to worry about following the sun's position and measuring shadows.

Chapter 2: Understanding the Components of Salah

Now that we're ready for Salah and facing the Qiblah, let's learn its components and the movements done during Salah. Salah is very simple. In this chapter, we'll discuss the positions you have to assume in Salah individually to clarify them. The actual steps will be discussed in the next chapter. This chapter will describe the positions in the same order they are supposed to be performed in Salah to better grasp the essence of the different movements. We will start with the physical movements, then the recitations, and then we'll put them together in the following chapter Insha'Allah.

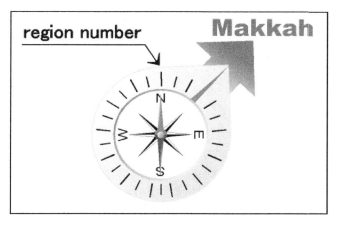

2. *To ensure you're facing Makkah, it's important to use a qibla compass. Source: https://commons.wikimedia.org/wiki/File:Qibla_compass.png*

Takbirat al Ihram

When you are standing, facing the Qiblah, of course, you raise your hands to the side of your head, preferably up to your ear lobes, and say "Allahu Akbar," meaning Allah (SWT) is The Greatest. This is called Takbirat al Ihram.

3. *Takbirat al Ihram position. Source: https://unsplash.com/photos/PXYJRuXC2Vg*

This way, you've started your Salah.

Qiyam

This is the posture of standing. You stand after saying Takbirat al Ihram with your hands folded over each other, the right always above the left, on your chest, and your eyes looking down at the ground at an angle. Remember not to look straight down; look at where your forehead will be during Sujud. Sujud will be explained shortly Insha'Allah. Your legs don't have to be too tight or too wide; they should be shoulder-width, or a little tighter is also good.

Ruku'

In this position, you are bending over with your back and arms straight and your palms on your knees, bowing essentially. Most people have their fingers pointing to their sides wrapped around their knees; however, pointing your fingers down at your feet is preferable.

Qaumah

Qaumah is the same as Qiyam. You stand back up after Ruku'. Before Ruku', you must have your hands folded on your chest. After Ruku', you can leave them at your sides or fold them on your chest; it is optional.

Sujud

After getting back up from Ruku and finishing your Qaumah, you go down to the ground performing Sujud. In Sujud, you bow low on the ground with both your hands and your knees touching the floor and your forehead and nose. Your toes should also be on the ground. The Prophet Muhammad (PBUH) has been reported to say: "When one of you prostrates, he should not kneel in the manner of a camel but should put down his hands before his knees." So, be careful to let your hands touch the ground before your knees do. Also, make sure that your toes touch the ground, as this is an essential part of prostration; Sujud is invalid without it. It is preferred if you can bend your toes under your feet, pointing them in the direction of the Qiblah, as this was the Sunnah of the Prophet Muhammad (PBUH). Remember not to let your forearms rest on the ground; for this position is similar to a dog sitting on the ground; your elbows should be at your sides, as Anas ibn Malik, one of the trusty companions of the Prophet (PBUH) has narrated that the Prophet Muhammad (PBUH) said: "Be straight in the prostrations and none of you should put his forearms on the ground (in the prostration) like a dog."

Juluus

Juluus, in Arabic, means sitting. In this position, you are simply sitting on the ground with your legs folded under you and your hands laying palms down at the ends of your thighs above your knees. The way your feet are positioned is up to you. You can keep both feet upright and sit on the backs of your heels with the balls of your feet on the ground supporting you. This is a valid way to sit. Following the Sunnah of the Prophet (PBUH), the better way is to keep your right foot upright with toes bent pointing at the Qiblah, lay your left foot under you, and sit on it. The second way, the one with the right foot upright and the left foot laid down, is the way the Prophet Muhammad (PBUH) sat most of the time, so it is best practice to do as he (PBUH) did. Both positions are with your knees in front of you and your feet under you; the only difference is the positioning of the feet. This covers all the physical positions you must assume during your Salah to Allah (SWT). Now, let's go over what you have to recite during Salah.

Reciting the Holy Qur'an

First and foremost, you start by reciting chapter 1 of the Holy Qur'an, Surah al-Fatihah. It is a Sunnah of the Prophet Muhammad (PBUH) to say *"A'uthu billahi min ashaitan irrajeem"* which means "I seek protection in Allah from Shaytan (the devil), the accursed one." before reciting Al-Fatihah, this is called Ta'awwudh. After Ta'awwudh, you do Tasmiyah, mentioning the name of Allah Almighty, by saying *"Bismillahir Rahmanir Raheem."* After that, you recite the seven Holy verses of Surah al-Fatihah, and then you say "Ameen":

"Al hamdu lil lahi rabbil 'alamin. Arrahmanir Rahim. Maliki yawmiddin. Iyyaka na'budu wa iyyaka nasta'in. Ihdinas siratal mustaqim. Siratal ladhina an'amta'alaihim, ghairil maghdubi'alaihim walad dhallin. (Ameen)"

Translation in English:

"All praises and thanks to Allah, the Lord of the worlds, the most Gracious, the most Merciful; Master of the Day of Judgment. You alone we worship; from You alone, we seek help. Guide us along the straight path – the path of those You favored, not those who earned Your anger or went astray."

You must recite Surah al-Fatihah in all Rak'ah of your Salah. Rak'ah will be shortly explained Insha'Allah.

After reciting Al-Fatihah, you recite any other passage from the Holy Qur'an. This differs between some Rak'ah and others, but this will also be explained shortly Insha'Allah. The length of the passage you recite is up to you; you could read three short verses (Ayah), one long Ayah, or the entire Surah al-Baqarah in one Rak'ah. The most common practice is to read one short Surah. Here is one example of a short Surah you could read:

"Bismillah Al-Rahman Al-Raheem

Qul Huwa-Allahu Ahad, Allahu El-Samad, Lam yalid wa lam yulad, Wa lam ya kun lahu kufuwan ahad."

This is the 112th chapter of the Holy Qur'an, Surah al-Ikhlas.

Translation in English:

"In the name of Allah, the Most Gracious, the Most Merciful. Say, He is Allah, the One. Allah is Eternal and Absolute. He begets not, nor was He begotten. And there is none co-equal unto Him."

Saying *"Bismillah Ar-Rahman Ar-Raheem"* before reciting the short Surah is optional. All these Surahs are recited during Qiyam when you are standing up after you say Takbirat al-Ihram.

Rak'ah

Rak'ah are units of Salah. They differ between different Salawat (plural of Salah), and it would be easier to explain them each with their respective Salah. The main difference is in the number of Rak'ah and certain movements done at the end of the second Rak'ah and sometimes the third and the fourth. The next chapter will make all these actions clearer and show the remaining parts in detail as well. These include Tasbih, Tashahhud, Taslim, and how different prayers like Fajr, Dhuhr, Maghrib, and Isha are prayed.

Chapter 3: Step-by-step Guide to Performing Salah

You've completed your wudu' and learned the basics. Now is the time for Salah. Salah is performed five times a day with different numbers of Rak'ah. Fajr, before dawn, has two, Dhuhr and Asr have four, Maghrib has three, and Isha has four. Let's see how every Rak'ah should go, and we'll discuss them chronologically with how the five prayers should be prayed.

4. Salah is performed in a specific way and the process is important to understand. Source: https://unsplash.com/photos/JHb1mRYJ11U

So, the first Salah is Fajr, prayed before dawn.

Fajr

#1: Intention

We've mentioned this with Wudu' and mention it here again to emphasize it more. Prophet Muhammad (PBUH) has been reported to say: "Deeds are but with intentions." You must intend from your heart to pray to Allah (SWT) for His satisfaction. This part is important not only to the purity of the intention but to the validity of your Salah. Your entire focus should be on the prayer and utterly nothing else. This is what's called Khushu'.

#2: Takbirat al Ihram

We've discussed this briefly in the previous chapter. You stand upright facing the Qiblah, raise your hands beside your earlobes, and say *"Allahu Akbar,"* which means "Allah is the Greatest." Right now, your prayer has officially begun. As we mentioned before, it is important to focus solely and wholeheartedly on prayer and ignore distractions as much as possible.

#3: Qiyam

Qiyam, as mentioned in the previous chapter, is standing upright with your back straight and your hands folded over your chest. Remember: the right over the left. Start by reciting Dua' al-Thana':

"Subhaanaka Allaahumma wa bihamdika, watabarakasmuka, wa ta'ala jadduka, wa laa 'ilaaha ghayruka." This means: "Glory and praise be to You, O Allah. Blessed be Your name and exalted be Your majesty,

there is none worthy of worship except You." You say Dua' al-Thana' only in the first Rak'ah.

Then, following the Sunnah of the Prophet (PBUH), you should say al Ta'awwudh:

"A'uthu billahi minash shaitanir rajeem."

This means: "I seek protection in Allah from Shaytan (the devil), the accursed one." After that, you do Tasmiyah; say "Bismillahir Rahmanir Raheem," and you start reciting Surat al-Fatihah:

"Al hamdu lil lahi rabbil 'alamin. Arrahmanir rahim. Maliki yawmiddin. Iyyaka na'budu wa iyyaka nasta'in. Ihdinas siratal mustaqim. Siratal ladhina an'amta'alaihim, ghairil maghdubi'alaihim wa lad dhallin. (Ameen)"

The translation of this was mentioned Alhamdulillah in the previous chapter. If you are praying alone, you must recite al-Fatihah in every Rak'ah of every Salah, obligatory or not.

Also, if you are praying alone, it is preferable, in Fajr, to recite the verses of the Qur'an out loud as this is the Sunnah of the Prophet Muhammad (PBUH). If you are praying behind an Imam and he recites loudly, saying "Ameen" after the Imam finishes reciting Surah al-Fatihah is sufficient. One thing you must never do is recite loudly along with the Imam.

Now, after reciting Surah al-Fatihah, since we are in the first Rak'ah in Fajr, you follow it by reciting a passage from the Holy Qur'an. You read this out loud as well. Length is not constricted at all; reading one or two verses or a full chapter is totally up to you. For Rak'ah, in which you will be reciting a passage of the Qur'an after al-Fatihah, here is an example of a short chapter of the Holy Qur'an:

"Inna a'taynakal Kawthar, fasalli lirabbik wa inhar, inna shani'aka huwal abtar"

This is the full chapter 108 Surah al-Kawthar, the shortest chapter in the Book of Allah (SWT), and here it is in English:

"Surely we have given you the Abundance; So, pray to your Lord and slaughter (the sacrifice). Surely your antagonist is he who is without offspring (lit. curtailed)."

#4: Ruku'

After you finish reciting, say "Allahu Akbar" once more and bow down, assuming the position of Ruku'. Bow down, put your hands on your knees in the manner we described before, and *say "Subhana Rabbiyal Adhim"* three times. This means: "How Perfect is my Lord, the Supreme. When you bow down, look at the place where your forehead will be during Sujud and keep your head in line with your back.

#5: Get Back up

Get back up from Ruku' to standing up straight again. As you get up say *"Sami'Allahu liman hamidah."* This means: "Allah hears those who praise Him." After that, you say, "Rabbana wa lakal hamd," which means: "Our Lord, praise be to You." If you are praying behind an Imam when he says *"Sami'Allahu liman hamidah,"* you don't have to say it; you can just say "Rabbana wa lakal hamd" when you get up.

#6: Sujud

After you say *"Rabbana wa lakal hamd"* standing straight, you go down to prostrate on the floor and say *"Allahu Akbar"* as you go down to the floor. Remember to put your hands down on the floor before your knees as the Prophet (PBUH) has instructed. Also, remember the seven parts of the body that are to touch the floor: the forehead, nose, knees, toes, and palms of your hands. Remember to keep your forearms off the ground and your elbows at your sides. Then, you say *"Subhana Rabiyal A'la"* three times. This means: "How Perfect is my Lord, the Highest."

5.   *Sujud. Source: https://www.pexels.com/photo/muslim-black-man-praying-at-home-5996991/*

Abu Hurayrah (may Allah be pleased with him), one of the closest companions of the Prophet Muhammad (PBUH), reported that the Prophet (PBUH) said: "The nearest a slave is to his Lord is when he is prostrating, so increase (your) supplications (while in this state)." Sujud is the best time to do Dua' (supplications), and Allah (SWT) says in Surah Ghafir chapter 40 verse 60: "And your Lord has said, "Invoke Me, and I will respond to you." This is the time for you to ask Allah (SWT) and remember He is the Most Generous and the Most Merciful.

#7: Juluus

After saying *"Subhana Rabiyal A'la"* three times, you get up from Sujud sitting on your left leg, as we discussed in the previous chapter. Your left foot rests on the floor, with your right foot upright and its toes pointing in the direction of the Qiblah. Don't forget to say *"Allahu Akbar"* on your way up. This is the Sunnah of the Prophet Muhammad (PBUH); however, it is OK if you wish to sit with both feet propped up. You place your hands, palms facing down near the end of your thighs, and you say, *"Rabbigh-fir lee,"* which means: "O my Lord, forgive me." You say this three times.

#8: Return to Sujud

After doing Juluus once, you go back down to the position of Sujud, like step #6, and say *"Subhana Rabiyal A'la"* three times and say your supplications if you wish. Now you have done Sujud twice and have completed your first Rak'ah. After your second Sajdah (the act of prostration means one prostration), you get back up to your feet, standing up straight with your hands folded on your chest, again right over left. Remember to say *"Allahu Akbar"* as you are getting up.

#9: The Second Rak'ah

After you've stood up, you start with Surah al-Fatihah again, just like the first Rak'ah, and you repeat all the previous steps except for Ta'awwudh and Dua' al-Thana'. After Surah al-Fatihah, you read another short passage from the Qur'an and are allowed to read the same verses you read from the previous Rak'ah. Then, you bow down in Ruku' and just repeat all the previous steps. The only difference comes after your second Sajdah.

#10: Al Tashahhud

Remember, we are now praying Fajr, which consists of two Rak'ah. And since you've done your second Sajdah, you are at the end of the prayer. The final step after your second Sajdah in your second Rak'ah is to sit back in Juluus position, just like you do between the two Sajdatayn (dual plural of Sajdah). Your feet are in the same position, and your palms are on your thighs. This time, you raise the index finger of your right hand.

And you say the following:

"At Tahiyyaatu lilaahi was Salawaatu wat tayibaatu

Assalaamu 'alaika ayyuhan nabiyyu wa rahmatu Allahi wa barakaatuh

Assalaamu 'alaynaa wa 'alaa 'ebaadillaahis saaliheen,

Ash hadu allaa ilaha illa Allah Wa ash hadu anna Muhammadan 'abduhuu wa rasuuluh,"

Then, you say:

"Allahumma salli 'ala Muhammadin wa 'ala aali Muhammad

Kamaa salayta 'ala Ibraaheem wa 'ala aali Ibrahim

Innaka Hameedun Majeed

Wa baarik 'ala Muhammadin wa 'ala aali Muhammad

Kamaa baarakta 'ala Ibraaheem wa 'ala aali Ibrahim

Innaka Hameedun Majeed"

This is the respective translation of both halves:

"All compliments, prayers, and pure words are due to Allah.

Peace be upon you, O Prophet, and the mercy of Allah and His blessings.

Peace be upon us, and on the righteous slaves of Allah.

I bear witness that none has the right to be worshipped except Allah, and I bear witness that Muhammad is His slave and Messenger"

"O Allah, send prayers upon Muhammad and upon the family (or followers) of Muhammad, Just as You sent prayers upon Ibrahim and the family (or followers) of Ibrahim,

Verily, you are full of Praise and Majesty.

O Allah, bless Muhammad and the family (or followers) of Muhammad as You blessed Ibrahim and the family (or followers) of Ibraaheem,

Verily, you are full of Praise and Majesty."

As this is Fajr prayer, you will be saying both the first and the second halves. After that, you look to your right and say: "Assalamu alaykum wa rahmatu Allah," and look to your left and say the same. This is called Tasleem, and it marks the end of your Salah. Congratulations! Now you have prayed, Fajr.

May Allah guide you and us to good and honest deeds.

Dhuhr

Dhuhr is the second prayer of the day, consisting of four Rak'ah. It is prayed at noon.

Note: The gap between Fajr and Dhuhr is the largest gap between two consecutive prayers throughout one day, sitting between about eight and nine hours in most countries. Now let's see how you pray, Dhuhr.

#1: The First Two Rak'atayn

The first two Rak'atayn (dual plural of Rak'ah in Arabic) of Dhuhr are similar to Fajr. You start with intention, of course, and after you say Takbirat al-Ihram, you can recite Dua' al-Thana': *"Subhaanaka Allaahumma wa bihamdika, watabarakasmuka, wa ta'aalaa jadduka, wa laa 'ilaaha ghayruka."*

Here it is in English: "All Glory be to You, O Allah! And Praise Be To You and Blessed Is Your Name and Exalted is Your Majesty and None has the Right to Be Worshiped Besides You."

Then, after Ta'awwudh: *"A'uthu billahi minash shaitanir rajeem,"* you recite Surah al-Fatihah and then a short passage from the Holy Qur'an. In Dhuhr, unlike Fajr, it is better to recite Surah al-Fatihah and a passage from the Holy Qur'an silently. You could simply recite them in a very low voice. From then on, you repeat the same steps as Fajr in the first two Rak'atayn. As we've explained, you should *"Allahu Akbar"* as you are going from each position to the next, except when you are going from Ruku' back to Qiyam, this is the only time you don't say "Allahu Akbar." Instead, you say *"Sami'Allahu liman hamidah."*

#2: The First Tashahhud

This step might make you wonder why it is called the 'first' Tashahhud? Well, in Fajr, since there are only two Rak'atayn, you only say Tashahhud once, and you say both of its halves. Dhuhr, however, consists of four Rak'ah So, after you get up from your second Sujud in the second Rak'ah of Dhuhr, you sit up in Juluus as usual, and you say only the first half of Tashahhud:

"At Tahiyyaatu lilaahi was Salawaatu wat tayibaatu

Assalaamu 'alaika ayyuhan nabiyyu wa rahmatu Allahi wa barakaatuh

Assalaamu 'alaynaa wa 'alaa 'ebaadillaahis saaliheen,

Ash hadu allaa ilaha illa Allah Wa ash hadu anna Muhammadan 'abduhuu wa rasuuluh,"

After that, you get back up to your feet, stand straight, and fold your hands over your chest. Remember to say "Allahu Akbar" as you are getting back up. Now you have finished half of Dhuhr, and you are starting your third Rak'ah.

#3: The Third Rak'ah

In the third Rak'ah, you start as usual. You say, *"Bismillahir Rahmanir Raheem,"* and you recite Surah al-Fatihah. Here is what's different in the third Rak'ah. You don't read a short passage from the Qur'an following Surah al-Fatihah. Remember, this is all still silent recitation, as this is Dhuhr. So, after you recite Surah al-Fatihah, you go straight to Ruku' and *say "Allahu Akbar"* as you go down. After that, you do Ruku' normally by saying: *"Subhana Rabiyal Adhim"* three times, then you get back up as you say *"Sami'Allahu liman hamidah."* Then after saying "Rabanna wa lakal hamd," you go down to Sujud while saying "Allahu Akbar" on the way down to your hands; remember to put your hands first as instructed by the Prophet (PBUH).

In Sujud, as usual, you say *"Subhana Rabiyal A'la"* three times, and you sit up to Juluus, don't forget the Takbir when you're transitioning from one move to another. During Juluus, you say "Rabigh-fir lee" three times, and then you go back down to your second Sujud.

#4: The Fourth Rak'ah

When you finish your second Sujud of your third Rak'ah, you get back up to Qiyam. Now, you've completed your third Rak'ah. It's time for your fourth and final Rak'ah of Salah al-Dhuhr. It is very similar to the third Rak'ah. You start by silently reciting Surah al-Fatihah in the Qiyam position, and you don't follow it with a passage from the Holy Qur'an, a short chapter, or anything. You simply go down straight to Ruku'.

As you've probably noticed, the steps starting from Ruku' are almost the same in all Rak'ah. So, after you get back up from Ruku', you go down to your first Sajdah, sit up in Juluus, and then go back down to your second Sajdah. During Ruku', you say: *"Subhana Rabiyal Adhim"* three times as usual. And when you get up from Ruku', after saying: *"Sami'Allahu liman hamidah,"* you say: *"Rabanna wa lakal hamd."* In Sujud, you say *"Subhana Rabiyal A'la"* three times, and between the two Sajdatayn, you say: *"Rabbigh-fer lee"* three times. Everything is like the previous Rak'ah. Again, don't forget to say *"Allahu Akbar"* when you are going from each position to the next, except when you are coming up from Ruku', say *"Sami'Allahu liman hamidah."* We will explain this briefly Insha'Allah.

After your second Sajdah of your fourth Rak'ah, now your Salah is coming to a close. This is the final step: You sit up in the Juluus position with your palms on your thighs and the right index finger raised. Then, you say the full Tashahhud - both halves:

"At Tahiyyaatu lilaahi was Salawaatu wat tayibaatu

Assalaamu 'alaika ayyuhan nabiyyu wa rahmatu Allahi wa barakaatuh

Assalaamu 'alaynaa wa 'alaa 'ebaadillaahis saaliheen,

Ash hadu allaa ilaha illa Allah Wa ash hadu anna Muhammadan 'abduhuu wa rasuuluh,"

Then, you say:

"Allahumma salli 'ala Muhammadin wa 'ala aali Muhammad

Kamaa salayta 'ala Ibraaheem wa 'ala aali Ibrahim

Innaka Hameedun Majeed

Wa baarik 'ala Muhammadin wa 'ala aali Muhammad

Kamaa baarakta 'ala Ibraaheem wa 'ala aali Ibrahim

Innaka Hameedun Majeed"

After that, you do Tasleem. You look to your right shoulder and say: *"Assalamu alaykum wa rahmatu Allah,"* then you look to your left shoulder and say the same again.

Congratulations again! Now, you have officially prayed, Dhuhr. May Allah (SWT) accept our prayers and guide you and us to more good and honest deeds.

Asr

Asr is the third prayer of the day. It consists of four Rak'aha, just like Dhuhr, and it is prayed in the same way. So, when you hear the Adhan (the call to prayer) for Asr, you pray in the same way as Dhuhr prayer. Remember the intention before anything, as the Prophet (PBUH) has said: "Deeds are but with intentions." We pray Asr in the afternoon when an object's shadow is exactly as long as it is.

Transitional Takbir

We have stressed multiple times before during the previous explanations on saying *"Allahu Akbar"* when you are going from one position to the next except for when you are coming back up from Ruku', for which you say: *"Sami'Allahu liman hamidah."* The action of saying *"Allahu Akbar"* is called Takbir, so the times you are saying *"Allahu Akbar"* between your moves is called Takbirat intiqaliyah, which literally means "Transitional Takbirs." Some schools of Fiqh, which is the study of Islamic jurisprudence, the applications of Shariaah, and a few more concepts in Islamic sciences, argue that Transitional Takbir must take up the entire time you are transitioning between positions exactly during that time. However, it is also okay to just say it as you transition between moves. You don't have to stress about starting to say it exactly as you begin moving from your current position and finishing it exactly as you stop moving and rest in your following position.

Abu Hurairah (May Allah be pleased with him) reported that the Prophet (PBUH) said: "The religion (of Islam) is easy, and whoever makes the religion a rigor, it will overpower him. So, follow a middle course (in worship); if you can't do this, do something near to it and give glad tidings and seek help (of Allah) at morning and at dusk and some part of night." This is one of the beauties of Islam, its ease.

Loud and Silent Recitation

We've talked earlier about how recitation should be aloud in Fajr and silent in Dhuhr. In which prayers do we recite loudly? And in which do we recite silently? The answer to this, as always, we take from the Sunnah of the Prophet (PBUH) as Allah (SWT) says in Surah al-Ahzab chapter 33 verse 21: "The Messenger of Allah is an excellent model for those of you who put your hope in God and the Last Day and remember Allah often." So, Prophet Muhammad (PBUH) has said: "Pray as you have seen me pray."

According to this, Salawat performed during the day are silent, and prayers performed during the night are when you recite loudly. This doesn't include special occasions like Salah al-Jumu'ah (the Friday prayer), Salah al-Eid (the prayer of Eid), and others. The five prayers we've mentioned: Fajr, Dhuhr, Asr, Maghrib, and Isha' are called Salah Fard, meaning they are obligatory. Other prayers are not obligatory. Salawat al-Sunnah, extra prayers done by the Prophet Muhammad (PBUH) other than the five Fard, are the most prominent example. Most Sunnah prayers consist of two Rak'atayn and are prayed just like Fajr, only at different times. We will discuss these extra prayers and other special ones in the final chapter of this book Insha'Allah.

Maghrib

Now that you've prayed Fajr, Dhuhr, and Asr Masha 'Allah, we've come to the fourth prayer of the day, Maghrib. Maghrib is one of the only prayers, Fard and otherwise, consisting of three Rak'ah, a generally uncommon number. We pray Maghrib at sundown and recite loudly. Here's how it goes:

#1: The First Two Rak'atayn

You pray the first two Rak'atayn normally as you would in Dhuhr and Asr. You start with intention, and after Takbirat al Ihram, then Dua' al-Thana' and Ta'awwudh. Then, you recite Surah al-Fatihah, aloud this time because this is Maghrib. Also note that the only thing that must be said aloud is the recitation of the Holy Qur'an, preferably Takbirat al Ihram and all Transitional Takbir. When you're saying *"Subhana Rabiyal Adhim"* during Ruku', for example, or *"Subhana Rabiyal A'la"* during Sujud, you don't have to say them out loud. The recitation of the Noble Qur'an is the most important.

#2: The Third Rak'ah

In Maghrib, like Dhuhr and Asr, you only say the first of Tashahhud after your second Sajdah in your second Rak'ah, and then you get up. In the third Rak'ah, you recite Surah al-Fatihah only. However, you recite it silently. Maghrib is a prayer in which you are supposed to recite aloud, but in the third Rak'ah, you recite silently. This is for recitation.

After silently reciting Surah al-Fatihah and getting up from your second Juluus in the second Rak'ah, you normally bow down in Ruku' and say *"Subhana Rabiyal Adhim"* three times. You come back up saying *"Sami'Allahu liman hamidah"* and say "Rabanna wa lakal hamd," then you go down to your first Sajdah.

You do your two Sajdatayn normally and then sit up after the second Sajdah. You say the full Tashahhud:

"At Tahiyyaatu lilaahi was Salawaatu wat tayibaatu

Assalaamu 'alaika ayyuhan nabiyyu wa rahmatu Allahi wa barakaatuh

Assalaamu 'alaynaa wa 'alaa 'ebaadillaahis saaliheen,

Ash hadu allaa ilaha illa Allah Wa ash hadu anna Muhammadan 'abduhuu wa rasuuluh,"

After that, the second half:

"Allahumma salli 'ala Muhammadin wa 'ala aali Muhammad

Kamaa salayta 'ala Ibraaheem wa 'ala aali Ibrahim

Innaka Hameedun Majeed

Wa baarik 'ala Muhammadin wa 'ala aali Muhammad

Kamaa baarakta 'ala Ibraaheem wa 'ala aali Ibrahim

Innaka Hameedun Majeed"

Then, you do Tasleem. You look to your right shoulder and say: *"Assalamu alaykum wa rahmatu Allah,"* then look to your left shoulder and say it again. This is how we pray, Maghrib.

May Allah (SWT) bless you and us with Jannah and guidance to the Right Path (the true path of Islam).

Isha'

After praying Maghrib, we have only one more Fard i.e., Isha'. Isha' is prayed when the night falls completely or when the white twilight is over. This is a little over an hour after Maghrib. So, when you hear the Adhan for Isha', here is what you do.

#1: The First Two Rak'atayn

As we hope you've gotten used to, the first two Rak'atayn are the same. After the true intention of praying to Allah (SWT), and after Takbirat al-Ihram, Dua' al-Thana', and Ta'awwudh, you recite Surah al-Fatihah and a passage from a Qur'an of your choice. Again, length is not an issue; read however long a passage suits you. In Isha', you recite loudly and say the first half of the Tashahhud after your second Sajdah of the second Rak'ah:

"At Tahiyyaatu lilaahi was Salawaatu wat tayibaatu

Assalaamu 'alaika ayyuhan nabiyyu wa rahmatu Allahi wa barakaatuh

Assalaamu 'alaynaa wa 'alaa 'ebaadillaahis saaliheen,

Ash hadu allaa ilaha illa Allah Wa ash hadu anna Muhammadan 'abduhuu wa rasuuluh,"

#2: The Second Two Rak'atayn

After you get up from your second Juluus in the second Rak'ah, you start reciting Surah al-Fatihah again. This is your third Rak'ah. As you did in Maghrib, you recite loudly only for the first two Rak'atayn, while in the third Rak'ah, you recite only Surah al-Fatihah silently. The fourth Rak'ah in Isha' is the same as well.

During the third Rak'ah, after your second Sajdah, you get up to the Qiyam position for the last time to start your fourth Rak'ah. Don't forget Transitional Takbir, of course. After you recite Surah al-Fatihah, bow down in Ruku' and say: *"Subhana Rabiyal Adhim"* three times. After that, get back up and say: *"Sami'Allahu liman hamidah,"* as you get up. Then, say: *"Rabanna wa lakal hamd"* and go down to Sujud.

Remember, in Sujud, your toes, knees, hands, forehead, and nose must all touch the ground. You say: *"Subhana Rabiyal A'la"* three times. This is your first Sajdah of the fourth Rak'ah. After this Sajdah, you sit up in the Juluus position and do Sujud one more time. Then, you sit up in Juluus one last time and say the full Tashahhud:

"At Tahiyyaatu lilaahi was Salawaatu wat tayibaatu

Assalaamu 'alaika ayyuhan nabiyyu wa rahmatu Allahi wa barakaatuh

Assalaamu 'alaynaa wa 'alaa 'ebaadillaahis saaliheen,

Ash hadu allaa ilaha illa Allah Wa ash hadu anna Muhammadan 'abduhuu wa rasuuluh,"

After that, the second half:

"Allahumma salli 'ala Muhammadin wa 'ala aali Muhammad

Kamaa salayta 'ala Ibraaheem wa 'ala aali Ibrahim

Innaka Hameedun Majeed

Wa baarik 'ala Muhammadin wa 'ala aali Muhammad

Kamaa baarakta 'ala Ibraaheem wa 'ala aali Ibrahim

Innaka Hameedun Majeed"

After that, you do Tasleem, and Congratulations!! You have prayed the five Fard prayers. May Allah (SWT) accept your and our good deeds and make our intentions pure.

Salah in the Mosque

Allah (SWT) says in Surah al-Baqarah chapter 2, verse 114: "And who is more unjust than he who prevents (praying in) the mosques of Allah so that His name be not mentioned in them, and endeavors (diligently) for their ruin? Those can in no way enter them except in fear, for them is disgrace in the present life, and in the Hereafter, they will have a tremendous torment." This calls us to stress on praying in mosques. The mosques of Allah are houses of worship and are meant to be prayed in. This, however, is for men only. Men are the only ones 'obliged' to pray in mosques. By obligation, we don't mean that it's ordained, but simply that it is only asked of men. Women are better advised to pray at home for their own protection, while men are encouraged to pray in mosques. Thus, we encourage you and ourselves to pray as much of the Fara'id (plural of Fard) prayers in mosques.

Manners in the Mosque

Now that we've said you should pray in a mosque. How should you? There are, of course, manners for praying and being in a mosque. First of all, take off your shoes before you go in. You will most likely find shelves to put your shoes on near the door Insha'Allah. Secondly, be careful not to make any noise as this may distract other people who are praying or may disturb others. Thirdly, you should pray two Rak'atayn. These are called Tahiyat al-Masjid (lit. the Salute of the Mosque). These are non-obligatory but preferable. These are prayed exactly like Fajr, although silently.

Now, onto the Fard prayers. When you are praying with a group of people, it is called Salah Jama'ah (lit. a group prayer). Prophet Muhammad (PBUH) has been reported to say: "Praying in congregation is twenty-five times better than praying alone." Another report says: "Twenty-seven." Despite the difference in numbers, both emphasize the virtue of Salah al-Jama'ah over performing Salah alone. The one leading the prayers is called the Imam; this is a great honor and is not earned easily. May Allah make you and us good examples to those aware of Him.

What's easier about Salah Jama'ah is that all you have to do is follow the Imam's movements. There are some differences between praying behind an Imam and praying alone.

While praying Salah alone, you are supposed to recite some parts loudly. However, when you are praying behind an Iman, it is only he who recites loudly. After the Imam finishes reciting Surah al-Fatihah, you must say Ameen, along with your brothers who are praying with you. After that, you listen to him reciting a passage of the Qur'an and follow along with his movements.

In fact, when you are praying behind an Imam in a congregation in a Salah with loud recitation, you do not recite at all. This follows Allah's command (SWT) as He says in Surah al-A'raf chapter 7 verse 204: "And when the Qur'an is read, then listen to it and hearken, that possibly you would be granted mercy." Otherwise, Salah behind an Imam is mostly the same. The Imam recites silently during Salah with silent recitation, and so do you. Just remember never to fall behind. And this is in Salah al-Jama'ah only. If you haven't finished reciting Surah al-Fatihah and the Imam says "Allahu Akbar" to go down to Ruku, you stop reciting, and you go with him. An Imam should normally be considerate in his pace of the people praying behind him but know this just in case.

Chapter 4: Common Mistakes in Salah

We've learned Alhamdulillah about Salah and how to perform it. However, there are some common mistakes that we should avoid. Some of these might even make your Salah unacceptable. Let's discuss these mistakes and how to avoid them.

Lack of Concentration

Allah (SWT) says in Surat al-Mu'minoon chapter 23, verses 1 and 2: "Successful indeed are the believers. Those who offer their Salah with all solemnity and full submissiveness." This is the meaning of Khushu'. Lack of concentration lies in a few things. Firstly, some people, may Allah guide us and them to the Right Path, look to their sides while praying if something catches their eye. This is fine if done by mistake but isn't if done on purpose. Some people, especially when they are among people who have been praying for many years, don't pay attention to the words they're saying because their minds are distracted or because Shaytan comes to them. You can avoid this by doing a few simple things. First of all, say

Ta'awwudh: *"A'uthu billahi minash shaitanir rajeem"* before starting your Salah and making Niyyah. Secondly, remember the Greatness of Allah (SWT) and the importance of standing in front of your Mighty Creator. Thirdly, you should choose a place without distractions and disturbance. Mosques are the best option for men, if available. However, a quiet room at home is the best option for women. For people who work under a manager, asking your manager for a quiet room to pray in is the best practice. Don't forget your intention before Salah, of course.

6. *A lack of concentration during prayer should be avoided at all costs. Source: https://www.pexels.com/photo/woman-in-black-hijab-sitting-beside-woman-in-black-hijab-7249338/*

Mispronunciation and Errors in Recitation

This issue is very controversial because it is a lot more common than initially perceived. A few mispronunciations by non-Arabic speakers are tolerable, but disregarding Tashkeel (Arabic diacritics) and sometimes the unwell memorization of the Holy Qur'an is malpractice. You must memorize Surah al-Fatihah well, as this is the one Surah that you read in all Salawat. After that, start by memorizing short Surahs of the Qur'an. Juz' 30 is a great place to start because it has the shortest chapters of the Holy Qur'an. If your first language isn't Arabic, you should ask Allah (SWT) for guidance and try to learn Arabic to the best of your abilities, as this can improve your recitation and understanding of the Holy Qur'an.

Mistakes, because they are unintentional by definition, don't invalidate your Salah. It's just important to be wary of them as avoiding them gets you closer to perfecting your Salah. Also, know that if you're praying behind an Imam with loud recitation and you hear them make a mistake, you are to correct them. You do that by simply saying the correct word he missed out loud; he should correct himself and reread the part he read wrong the first time. This is one of the simplest mistakes to avoid, so don't stress about it and try learning proper pronunciation to please Allah (SWT). May Allah (SWT) bless you and us with his Infinite Mercy.

Rushing through Salah

This is one of the most common mistakes among many Muslims, may Allah (SWT) guide them and us to His Right Path. Allah (SWT) says in Surah al-Muzammil chapter 73 verse 4: "And recite the Qur'an (aloud) in a slow, (pleasant tone and) style." Take your time with Salah. You stand praying to the Creator of the Universe; mind your situation well. You don't have to prolong Salah, but absolutely do not rush it. Rushing is an issue because of many things. Firstly, it doesn't show your respect to the Salah and to the fact you're standing before Allah (SWT). Secondly, it generates more mistakes. You might not pay proper attention to your recitation and your words, and you might miss something.

Recite the Qur'an carefully and ponder the meanings of Allah's Holy Word (SWT). Give Salah its justice. Pronounce every word to its fullest. Say: *"Subhana Rabiyal Adhim"* and *"Subhana Rabiyal A'la"* without speeding through them. You must achieve calmness and tranquility in your Salah. Breathe with every movement, and remember you stand before Allah Almighty. Nothing could be more important. Don't worry about anything around you. Don't worry about returning to your desk, as this might be common with people who have to pray while working. Remember that rushing Salah is also an attribute of Munafiqin (Hypocrites), so please be careful.

Incomplete or Incorrect Performance

This mistake happens quite often, although not as common as the ones mentioned above. First of all, any willful violation of any Wajib act in Salah invalidates that. Wajib acts are compulsory ones, so reciting Surah al-Fatihah, for example, is a Wajib. Takbirat al-Ihram is a Wajib act, so are Sujud and Ruku'. Wajib acts define Salah, so any violation of them can invalidate your Salah.

On the other hand, one might simply forget something; we are only human, after all. A common mistake is forgetting to sit up for the first Tashahhud in the second Rak'ah of Salawat with four Rak'ah: Dhuhr, Asr, and Isha'. One could simply get up quickly. If this is an honest mistake, then it's fine. Remember that Allah (SWT) is the Most Merciful and that His religion is one of ease.

Let's look at a situation where you unintentionally miss an action or position. Let's say you are praying, Asr, and you are in your first Rak'ah. You are doing your first Sajdah, and after saying *"Subhana Rabiyal A'la"* three times, you get up right away. Then, later on in your Salah, you remember that you missed your second Sajdah in the first Rak'ah. You continue praying normally until your last Rak'ah; after your second Sajdah, you say the full Tashahhud normally, but then you don't do Taslim immediately. You bow down in Sujud, say: *"Subhana Rabiyal Adhim"* three times, and sit back in Juluus. In this Juluus, you say: "Rabbigh-fer lee" three times, as usual, and you go back down for one more Sajdah, and you say: "Subhana Rabiyal Adhim" three times again. After that, you get up and do Tasleem immediately, ending your Salah. The two Sajdatayn you just did are called Sajdatayn Sahw; Sahw translates to inattention or oversight. This way, your Salah is valid. But remember, it must be an honest mistake, you can't miss a move on purpose thinking you're just going to do two Sajdatayn Sahw, and that's it. Sajdatayn Sahw is for when you truly forget. This way, you've learned about some of the most common mistakes in Salah. Make sure to avoid them, may Allah (SWT) bless you and us with his Infinite Mercy.

Chapter 5: Enhancing the Quality of Salah

We've talked about the common mistakes made during Salah and how to avoid them. Now, how do we make our Salah better in order to please Allah (SWT) more? How do we get closer to our Creator with our Salah?

Khushu'

Khushu' is one of the most important aspects of your Salah. In simple terms, Khushu' is focusing on your Salah and only that. Remember, you stand before the Almighty Rahman and act accordingly. It is reported that 'Abdullah ibn Abbas, one of the companions of the Prophet (PBUH), said: "Two Rak'ah with contemplation are better than standing for the entire night with an inattentive heart." Salah is not a charade or a sequence of movements. It is time you take out of your day to obey Allah (SWT) and connect with Him. To try and attain this, it is important to be calm and don't rush your Salah. Servitude to Allah (SWT) has its sweetness; savor it. Vary the Surahs you read after Surah al-Fatihah; this helps you stay more focused. This also pushes you to memorize more of the

Holy Qur'an, so it's a win on two fronts. Last but not least, understand what you are saying. Allah (SWT) urges Muslims to ponder his Holy Book, so do that, and you shall Insha'Allah find in it beauty and the Infinite Wisdom of Allah (SWT). May I remind you that Allah (SWT) says in Surah al-A'raf chapter 7, verse 204: "And when the Qur'an is read, then listen to it and hearken, that possibly you would be granted mercy."

Beautifying Recitation

Prophet Muhammad (PBUH) has been reported to say: "Beautify the Qur'an with your voices." And he also said: "He who does not recite the Qur'an melodiously is not one of us." If you've heard any Qari' (lit. reader in Arabic) of the Holy Qur'an, you probably know about this. Try listening to Qura' (plural of Qari') and see how they read. Listen well, imitate them, and live with the Ayah (verses). You must know how different it is to listen to an Ayah recited like that and when you simply read it normally. The difference is vast. Here are some recommendations for skillful Qura' of the Holy Qur'an: the Saudi Abu Bakr Shatri, the Egyptian Abdul Basit Abdul Samad, and the Egyptian Muhammad Al-Minshawi. You don't have to stick to the style of one Qari'; of course, develop your own voice. Learn Tajwid and know how to recite and pronounce it beautifully. You could try reciting the Qur'an daily and listening to Qura' as well. When you make this a habit, you'll find your voice getting better and better sooner or later Insha'Allah. But remember to have patience and work for it, may Allah (SWT) bless you and us with his Infinite Mercy.

7. *Beautifying your recitation allows you to focus on the Salah.*
Source: https://www.pexels.com/photo/close-up-photo-of-pages-of-the-holy-quran-with-prayer-beads-6920597/

Strengthening Your Spirituality

In earlier chapters, we talked a lot about intention before your actions and your deeds towards Allah (SWT). This serves to remind you, as well, of our main purpose. We do Salah to please Allah (SWT); remember this in all of your actions, not just Salah. When done correctly, this provides a sense of peace and truth you cannot imagine. Allah (SWT) says in Surah Muhammad chapter 47, verse 2: "And the ones who have believed and done deeds of righteousness and have believed in what has been successively sent down upon Muhammad, and it is the Truth from their Lord-He will expiate for them their odious deeds and will make righteous their state."

Before you go into Salah, think about where you're going for a moment. You stand before Allah (SWT), reciting his

Holy Word, contemplating it, and pondering its meanings. In the simple movements of Salah, you connect with Allah (SWT) in a manner unlike any other deed in all of Islam. During Sujud, you do Dua' asking the mercy of Allah (SWT). During Juluus, you ask Him (SWT) for forgiveness. During Ruku' and Sujud, you mention and glorify His name: *"Subhana Rabiyal Adhim," "Subhana Rabiyal A'la."* Think about every one of these movements and what it means in your relationship with Allah (SWT).

Seeking Knowledge and Understanding the Meaning

This part is the most exciting, in a sense. As we've said before, you must ponder the Noble Qur'an and contemplate its Holy Ayah. This is important during Salah and when reading the Qur'an in general. Allah (SWT) says in Surah Sad chapter 38 verse 29: "A Book We have sent down to you, Blessed, that they may ponder over its Ayah (verses, signs) and that men endowed with intellects would remind themselves." Think about the deeper meaning of each verse you recite in your Salah: the Ayah about Jannah, the Ayah with commandments.

A common question in this area is: "How?" Take the Ayah with Jannah, for example. When you recite them in Qiyam and go down to Sujud, ask Allah (SWT) for Jannah in your Dua'. For Ayah, with commandments, think to yourself, "Do I do this? Am I following this correctly?" Try reading Tafsir. This helps tremendously with seeking knowledge and understanding of the Qur'an and shall Insha'Allah, make your Salah better.

We've learned how to enhance our Salah and be closer to Allah (SWT) during our prayers. Earlier, we mentioned that there are Salah that are different from the regular Fard. Let's talk about them in the next chapter.

Chapter 6: Salah in Special Circumstances

The only obligatory Salawat in Islam are the five Fard: Fajr, Dhuhr, Asr, Maghrib, and Isha'. However, other Salawat besides these can bring you closer to Allah (SWT) Insha'Allah if you do them. Let's know them.

Salah al-Jumu'a

8. *The Friday prayer is usually done in a group at the mosque. Source: https://unsplash.com/photos/Y2oE2uNLSrs*

This literally means the Friday prayer. Salah al-Jumu'a is only a different form of Dhuhr; Dhuhr is prayed differently on Fridays. These are its steps:

#1: Khutbah

Khutba is a sermon given by the Imam of the mosque every Friday right after the Adhan of Dhuhr. It is obligatory for men to attend it at the mosque, for men who can, so young children below the age of puberty are exempted from the obligation, and so are elders incapable of going out. This sermon focuses on a certain topic, mostly something contemporary. The news of the Muslim Ummah (lit. nation in Arabic) is a popular topic. A Khutbah could be about a Hadith of the Prophet Muhammad (PBUH) or an Ayah of the Holy Qur'an. The topic is up to the Imam, giving the Khutbah to choose, but you are to listen intently. May Allah (SWT) grant us His infinite mercy.

#2: Two Rak'atayn

This is the major difference in Dhuhr of Friday. After hearing the Khutbah, you pray two Rak'atayn behind the Imam. These two Rak'atayn, however, are with loud recitation. Since you are praying behind an Imam, you are to listen and say *"Ameen"* when he finishes Surah al-Fatihah. Don't forget your intention before you start your Salah.

After Surah al-Fatihah and the short passage of the Qur'an, you do Ruku' normally, followed by Qiyam again. After that you do Sujud and so on. In the second Sajdah of the second Rak'ah, you say the full Tashahhud:

"At Tahiyyaatu lilaahi was Salawaatu wat tayibaatu

Assalaamu 'alaika ayyuhan nabiyyu wa rahmatu Allahi wa barakaatuh

Assalaamu 'alaynaa wa 'alaa 'ebaadillaahis saaliheen,

Ash hadu allaa ilaha illa Allah Wa ash hadu anna Muhammadan 'abduhuu wa rasuuluh,"

After that, the second half:

"Allahumma salli 'ala Muhammadin wa 'ala aali Muhammad

Kamaa salayta 'ala Ibraaheem wa 'ala aali Ibrahim

Innaka Hameedun Majeed

Wa baarik 'ala Muhammadin wa 'ala aali Muhammad

Kamaa baarakta 'ala Ibraaheem wa 'ala aali Ibrahim

Innaka Hameedun Majeed"

You follow that by Tasleem: "Assalamu 'alaykum wa Rahmat Ullah" to your right shoulder once and then to your left shoulder. This is how you pray, Salah al-Jumu'a. For people who don't pray Jumu'a at the mosque, they just pray Dhuhr normally. Please consider well your excuse for not attending, as the Khutbah is part of the Fard.

Salah al-Musafir

This means the Traveler's prayer. Often during travel, people are tired, especially if their traveling takes numerous hours, but Allah (SWT) has given His religion, Islam, the attribute of ease, so when you are traveling, Salah is a little shorter.

Dhuhr and Asr

Dhuhr and Asr are shortened to two Rak'atayn each instead of four. You are allowed to join them and pray both at the time of Dhuhr. So, when you hear the Adhan of Dhuhr, you pray two Rak'atayn silently, and that's Dhuhr. Then, right after Tasleem from these two Rak'atayn, you get up to pray two more Rak'atayn; these are for Asr. This way, when you hear Asr, you don't pray it again. This is, of course, supposing you are traveling at that exact time. You should only do this joining, known as Jam' (lit. joining in Arabic) when it is too difficult to pray the two prayers apart.

Maghrib and Isha'

Maghrib and Isha' are also shortened to two Rak'atayn each but are both prayed in the time of Isha,' the later one's time instead of the earlier one. So, when you hear the Adhan for Isha', you pray two Rak'atayn. That's Maghrib. Then, two more. That is Isha'. Again, Jam' is only advised when it is too difficult to pray the prayers apart.

Fajr

As Fajr is already two Rak'atayn, you can't shorten it further, and you have to pray it on time.

Keep in mind that this is a license given by Allah (SWT). Your Salah is shorter in length but as complete a deed as a normal Salah. Prophet Muhammad (PBUH) has been reported to say: "Allah (SWT) loves that His permissions be practiced, just as he dislikes that disobedience to Him be committed." Allah (SWT) has given you this permission, so use it as He is pleased to make servitude easier for Muslims.

A traveler is granted this permission if his traveling distance is 50 miles or more, which is about 80 kilometers. If you don't intend to stay at the place you've traveled to, you intend to leave as soon as your business is finished; you are allowed Qasr (shortening Salah) until you leave the place you've traveled to. If you intend to stay for more than four days, you are to perform the full Salawat.

Salah al-Janazah

Janazah literally means funeral in Arabic. Funeral prayers include no Ruku' and no Sujud and are always prayed silently regardless of the time of the day. They consist of four Takbirat (plural of one Takbirah, which is when you say "Allahu Akbar").

#1: Takbirat al-Ihram

You stand up in Qiyam and you say "Allahu Akbar", raising your hands to the sides of your ears. After that all you do is recite Surah al-Fatihah:

"Al hamdu lil lahi rabbil 'alamin. Arrahmanir rahim. Maliki yawmiddin. Iyyaka na'budu wa iyyaka nasta'in. Ihdinas siratal mustaqim. Siratal ladhina an'amta'alaihim, ghairil maghdubi'alaihim wa lad dhallin. (Ameen)"

#2: The Second Takbirah

After Surah al-Fatihah, you say *"Allahu Akbar"* once more while still standing up in Qiyam position. You don't go down to do Ruku'. After this Takbirah, you say the second half of the Tashahhud:

"Allahumma salli 'ala Muhammadin wa 'ala aali Muhammad

Kamaa salayta 'ala Ibraaheem wa 'ala aali Ibrahim

Innaka Hameedun Majeed

Wa baarik 'ala Muhammadin wa 'ala aali Muhammad

Kamaa baarakta 'ala Ibraaheem wa 'ala aali Ibrahim

Innaka Hameedun Majeed"

#3: The Third Takbirah

After that, you say "Allahu Akbar" one more time. Now, you do Dua' for the deceased, asking Allah (SWT) Jannah and Mercy for them. A good Dua' is:

"Allahuma igh-fir lahu wa irhamh birahmatika ya Arham ar-Rahimeen" if it's a male, and *"Allahuma igh-fir laha wa irhamha birahmatika ya Arham ar-Rahimeen"* if it's a female.

The former means: "O Allah, the Most Merciful of the merciful, forgive him and bless him with Your Mercy," and the latter means: "O Allah, the Most Merciful of the merciful, forgive her and bless her with Your Mercy."

#4: The Fourth Takbirah

After that, you say *"Allahu Akbar"* one last time and do Dua' for yourself and all Muslims. You could say: *"Allahuma igh-fir lana wa irhamna birahmatika ya Arham ar-Rahimeen,"* which means: "O Allah, the Most Merciful of the merciful, forgive us and bless us with Your Mercy."

After that, you do Tasleem. You look to your right shoulder, remember you are still standing up, and say: *"Assalamu 'alaykum wa Rahmat Ullah,"* then look to your left shoulder and say the same.

If you are praying behind an Imam, which is more likely in Salawat al-Janazah, follow the Takbirat of the Imam. Even if you haven't finished Surah al-Fatihah after the first Takbirah and the Imam does the second Takbirah, do the second Takbirah and start the second half of the Tashahhud and so on. You must raise your hands to the sides of your ears during the first Takbirah, Takbirat al-Ihram, while it is an option in the following Takbirat; you may raise your hands or not, but you have to say *"Allahu Akbar."*

Salah al-Eid

Salah al-Eid is prayed twice a year. The first is on the first day of Eid al-Fitr, on the first day of the month of Shawwal, which comes after Ramadan, and the second is on the first day of Eid al-Adha, on the tenth of the month of Dhul' Hijja. Salah al-Eid consists of only two Rak'atayn and is very simple. It is the same for both Eids. It is prayed in the very early morning, shortly after dawn.

#1: Clothing and Takbirat

First of all, it is of the Sunnah of the Prophet Muhammad (PBUH) to wear nice clothes, especially on the occasion of Eid. Most people buy new clothes for themselves and their loved ones, which is even better. On the day of Eid, you will most likely hear Takbirat al-Eid coming from mosques around you.

"Allahu Akbar, Allahu Akbar, Allahu Akbar, La Ilaha illa Allah

Allahu Akbar, Allahu Akbar wa lillah al-Hamd"

It is Sunnah to do these Takbirat along with the mosque at home, on the street, in your car, or anywhere as long as it is the day of Eid before Salah al-Eid.

#2: Takbirat of the First Rak'ah

What is different about Salah al-Eid is the number of Takbirat. Salah al-Eid has a total of twelve major Takbirat. In the first Rak'ah, you start with Takbirat al-Ihram. *"Allahu*

Akbar," then you say *"Allahu Akbar"* again six more times. That is a total of seven. This is for the first Rak'ah. As this Salah is prayed at the mosque, you must follow the Imam. After that, Surah al-Fatihah comes normally, a short passage, and then Ruku' and Sujud as usual. This Salah has loud recitation, so all you have to do is say *"Ameen"* after the Imam finishes Surah al-Fatihah and listen as he recites the short passage of the Holy Qur'an. Keep in mind that this is still a Salah to Allah (SWT), so focus on the Ayah.

#3: The Second Rak'ah

The second Rak'ah starts with the Transitional Takbir from the Sujud of the first Rak'ah, as usual, and then you add four more Takbirat for a total of five. In both Rak'atayn, you raise your hands to the sides of your ears with every Takbirah.

Taraweeh

Taraweeh prayers are one of the special features of the Sacred Month of Ramadan. Taraweeh prayers are prayed at night, right after Isha', and have loud recitations. They are normally prayed in sets of two Rak'atayn and only in Ramadan. There is no actual constraint on the number of Rak'ah you pray as long as you pray them two at a time. Mosques generally tend to do eight; four sets of two, with a break between the first four and the second four. This break is sometimes only a few minutes long for the Imam and the people praying behind him to rest, and then Salah commences right away once again, and sometimes there is a short Khutbah given by the Imam. This Khutbah is shorter than the Khutbah of Jumu'ah, and the topics are generally more compact.

It is up to you to pray Taraweeh at home or at the mosque. Again, pray for as long as you like. Prophet Muhammad (PBUH) has been reported to say: "Choose such actions as you are capable of performing, for Allah (SWT) does not grow weary. The most beloved religion to Him is that in which a person persists." As long as your intention is the satisfaction of Allah (SWT), do what you can and do not push yourself, for Islam is a religion of ease.

Each two of the Raka'ah you pray in Taraweeh are identical to Fajr, except for the timing. You start with the intention of praying Taraweeh, then you do Takbirat al-Ihram, Dua' al-Thana', Ta'awwudh, and start reciting Surah al-Fatihah and so on until you say the full Tashahhud after the second Sajdah of the second Rak'ah, then you do Tasleem. After that, you get up and pray another two Rak'atayn, and so on. If you go to pray at a mosque and you wish to pray with the Imam for only the first two or four, for example, you are allowed to leave after you achieve the number you desire. Just know that this is a tremendous chance to get closer to Allah (SWT) as the recitation of the Qur'an during Taraweeh is often preferred lengthier, and you get to listen more of the Qur'an and ponder and think more.

Salah During Illness

When we fall ill, Salah is often not easily performed. However, Allah (SWT) has made Islam a religion of ease, and in whatever state you are in, you are allowed to pray. If you can't pray standing up, you can pray sitting. If you can't pray sitting, you can pray lying on your side. May Allah (SWT) protect us and all Muslims from all forms of illness.

#1: Sitting

If you can't stand, sit on a chair in the direction of Qiblah with your back propped up as much as you can and fold your hands over your chest, and your feet should be flat on the floor. This position replaces Qiyam, so in this position, you do Takbirat al-Ihram, recite Dua' al-Thana, and then recite Surah al-Fatihah, and a short passage of the Qur'an.

#2: Ruku' and Sujud while sitting

When you go down for Ruku', bend down simply while you are still sitting and put your hands on the place they're supposed to normally be during Juluus and say: *"Subhana Rabiyal Adhim"* three times, as usual.

When you return from Ruku', sit up while still on the chair. After that, for Sujud, bend down the same way you did when doing Ruku' and say: *"Subhana Rabiyal A'la"* three times. For Juluus, you sit back up and say*: "Rabigh-fer lee"* three times and go down for Sujud again. After this Sajdah, you get back up to your sitting position and start reciting Surah al-Fatihah again for the second Rak'ah. This is how you pray one Rak'ah when you can't stand up. It is permissible to do with any Fard prayer, but you cannot shorten the number of Rak'ah; you have to pray the same number of Rak'ah.With this, we conclude our book. May Allah (SWT) guide you and us to good deeds in the present and the future, and May He forgive us for our sins.

Assalamu 'alaykum wa Rahmatullahi Wa Barakatuh.

References

Beginner's Guide to Learning How to Pray Salah. (n.d.). My Masjid. https://www.mymasjid.ca/beginners-guide-learn-pray-salah/

Constituent Parts of Prayer. (n.d.). Al Islam. https://www.alislam.org/book/salat/constituent-parts-of-prayer/

How to Perform Prayer (Salah). (n.d.). Dar Al-Iftaa. https://www.dar-alifta.org/en/article/details/250/how-to-perform-prayer-salah